For
Emma, Elsie
and Emile
M. R.

For Katie
C. R.

THIS
BOOK
belongs to:

....

....

....

A GREAT BIG CUDDLE

Poems for the Very Young

Michael Rosen illustrated by **Chris Riddell**

CANDLEWICK PRESS

CONT

eNTs

TIPPY-TAPPY

Tippy-tappy
Tippy-tappy
Tap, tap, tap.

Dippy-dippy
Dippy-dippy
Dip, dip, dip.

Nippy-nappy
Nippy-nappy
Nap, nap, nap.

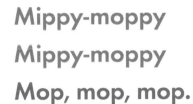

Mippy-moppy
Mippy-moppy
Mop, mop, mop.

Stippy-steppy
Stippy-steppy
Step, step, step.

Hippy-hoppy
hippy-hoppy
Hop, hop, hop.

Pippy-peppy
Pippy-peppy
Pep, pep, pep.

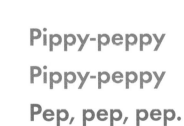

Kippy-cuppy
Kippy-cuppy
Cup, cup, cup.

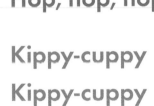

Lippy-lippy
Lippy-lippy
Lip, lip, lip.

Ippy-uppy
Ippy-uppy
Up, up, up.

THE BUTTON BOP

Top button

Bottom button

Top button

Top.

Bottom button

Top button

Bottom button

Bop.

Top, top

Bottom button top

Bop, bop

Bottom button bop.

PARTY TIME

Ten ten
Where? When?

Nine nine
Are we on time?

Eight eight
Are we late?

4

Seven seven

Is this heaven?

Six six

How's tricks?

Five five

Who's arrived?

Four four

Who's at the door?

Three three

Is it me?

Two two

Is it you?

One one

The cake's done.

BOING!

Boing! Boing!

Bounce bounce.

I'm a ball

Bounce bounce.

BOING!

Jump jump

Pounce pounce.

I'm a tiger

Pounce pounce

ROARRRRRR!

MUSIC

Rumba

Ya-rumba

Rumba-rumba-bumba

Bumba

Ya-bumba

Bumba-bumba-rumba

Rumba Ya-rumba
Rumba-rumba-bumba
Bumba Ya-bumba
Bumba-bumba-rumba

If you really want to prove it

Listen to the music

If you really want to lose it

Listen to the music

If you really want to use it

Listen to the music

You really can't refuse it

Listen to the music

I WENT

I went to Lapland

I saw a reindeer on the loose.

I went to Canada

I saw a chocolate mousse.

I went to the river

I saw a big green frog.

I went to New York

I saw a hot dog.

WIGGLY WIGGLY

Jiggle jiggle, we're all wriggly

Wriggle wriggle, we're all wiggly

Wiggle wiggle, we're all giggly

Giggle giggle, we're all jiggly.

Jiggly jiggly,

wriggly wriggly,

wiggly wiggly, giggly giggly.

14

WHY?

Why did the man bend down low?

Why did the man eat some snow?

Why did the man get up and go?

Why did the man walk very slow?

Why did the man say, "I don't know"?

LOST

One moment they were there and we were having fun.

Now they've disappeared, every single one.

I don't know where to go and I'm feeling rather scared.

I don't know where they are, it's not as if they cared.

I'm lost, I'm lost, I'm halfway up the stairs.

They've only gone and left me, and nobody cares.

Help me, help me, someone. Can't you hear me shout?

Isn't anybody here who can come and help me out?

I'm alone and lonely and it's starting to get dark.

Where is everyone? Did they go to the park?

Are they in or out? Did they go up to town?

Do you think I should go upstairs? Or down?

I don't know, I don't know, anything at all.

I'm going to sit still now and just look at the wall.

FLYING

We've got legs.

We've got feet.

See us walking

Down the street.

If we had wings,

We could fly.

See us flying

In the sky.

We look down.

See the street.

Look at us.

See our feet.

We're in the street.

See the sky.

We can't see us,

Even if we try.

READING LESSON

This is how you read:

Can you see?

This says "you."

This says "me."

When you see "me"

You say "me."

When you see "you"

Say "you"—do you see?

All together now.

Can you see?

You, you, you.

Me, me, me.

Well done all.

That's it for today. You can all read.

You can go and play.

FINGER STORY

Fingers in bed

Fingers wake up

Fingers stretch

Fingers shake up

Fingers cut

Fingers bread

Fingers butter

Fingers spread

Fingers go out

Fingers walk

Fingers wave

Fingers talk

Fingers climb

Fingers mountain

Fingers slide

Fingers fountain

Fingers run

Fingers jump

Fingers fall

Fingers bump

Fingers home

Fingers bread

Fingers tired

Fingers bed.

WHAT A FANDANGO!

A mango met a mango

And they started to tango

In the market not far from here.

Now we all do the tango

What a fandango!

In the market not far from here.

LUNCHTIME

Time for lunch

Munch munch

Time for a munch

Crunch crunch

Munch munch

Crunch crunch

Munchy munchy

Crunchy crunchy

I AM HUNGRY

I am hungry • really hungry • hungry,
hungry, hungry. I'm so hungry
I'll eat a cheese roll • Cornflakes in a bowl
A plate of fried rice • Two chocolate mice
A slice of toast • A Sunday roast
A vanilla ice cream • A very bad dream
A gingerbread man • A frying pan
A piece of cake • A headache
A giant prune • A bit of the moon
Some fried fish • A birthday wish
A real live mouse • The side of a house
An egg yolk • A funny joke
The egg white • A dark and stormy night
A plastic tray • One fine day
A television show • The sound of no
A game of chess • The sound of yes
One pea • Then I'll eat me.

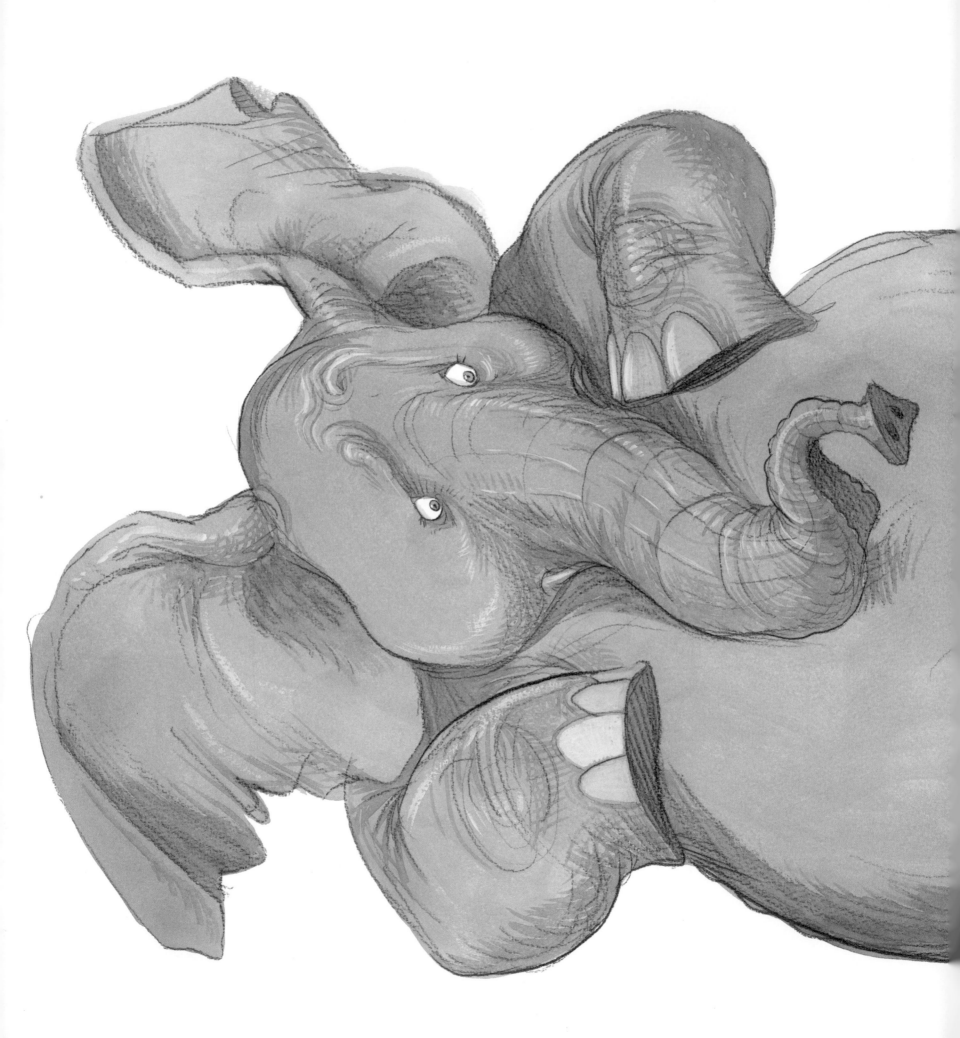

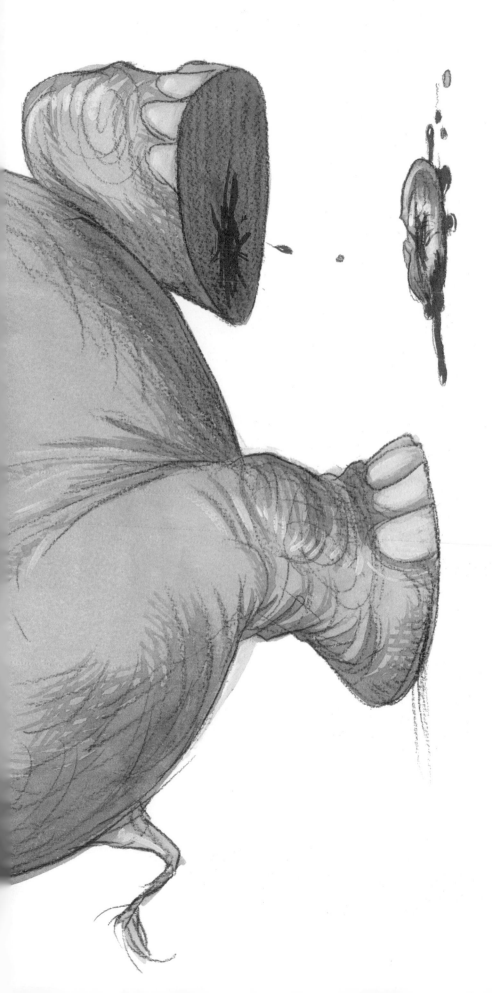

DON'T SQUASH

Don't squash your toes, Doris,
don't squash your toes.
Don't squash your nose, Doris,
don't squash your nose.

Don't squash your bun, Doris,
don't squash your bun.
Don't squash the sun, Doris,
don't squash the sun.

Don't squash cars, Doris,
don't squash cars.
Don't squash the stars, Doris,
don't squash the stars.

Don't squash the fly, Doris,
don't squash the fly.
Don't squash the sky, Doris,
don't squash the sky.

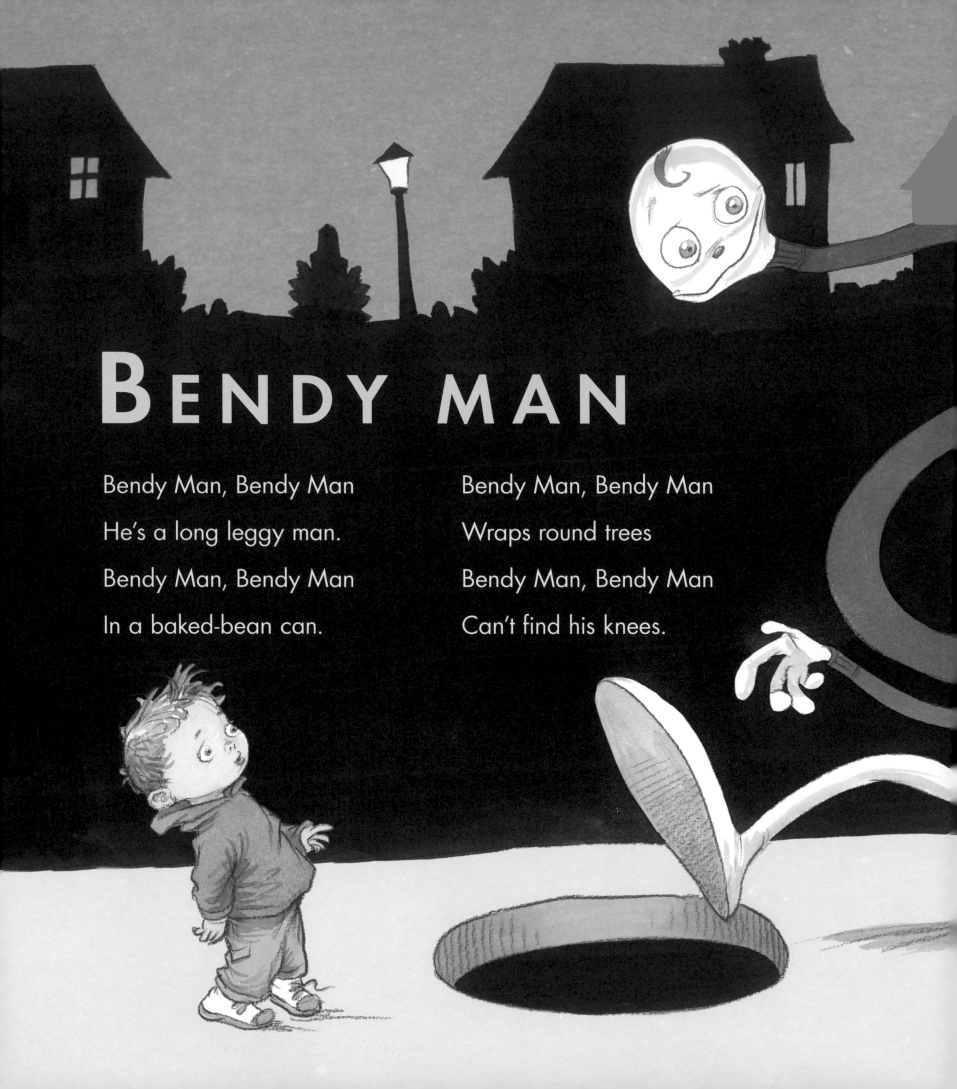

BENDY MAN

Bendy Man, Bendy Man

He's a long leggy man.

Bendy Man, Bendy Man

In a baked-bean can.

Bendy Man, Bendy Man

Wraps round trees

Bendy Man, Bendy Man

Can't find his knees.

Bendy Man, Bendy Man
Creeps round town
Bendy Man, Bendy Man
Creeps underground.

Bendy Man, Bendy Man
Under the bridge
Bendy Man, Bendy Man
Sitting in the fridge.

Bendy Man, Bendy Man
Bends in two
Bendy Man, Bendy Man
Asleep in a shoe.

ONCE

Once upon a plom

There lived a poor little mom

Along with her children three.

There was a great big Gom

A Flom and a Chom

Who all sang, "Me, me, me."

Then the Flom said, "Ping!"

And the Chom said, "Ting!"

And the Gom said, "Ping Pong Pee."

And the poor little mom

Said to the Gom,

"What about me, me, me?"

Now along came a Berrible.

This Berrible was terrible.

It roared like the stormy sea:

"Out the way, Gom,

The Flom and the Chom!

Your mom is dinner for me!"

"You can't eat Mom,"

Said the great big Gom.

"Oh no!" they said all three.

So they gobbled up the Berrible,

Who tasted really terrible.

Now they're happy as happy can be.

MR. HOBSON-
JOBSON SAYS:

Itty-bitty • Bat • Tittle-tattle • Tat

Shilly-shally • Shout • Dilly-dally • Out

Willy-nilly • Woo • Silly Billy • Boo!

Roly-poly • Rip • Pitter-patter • Pip

Wibble-wobble • Woe • Namby-pamby • No

Hunky-dory • Hop • Topsy-turvy

Stop

I AM

ANGRY

I am angry • really angry • angry,
angry, angry. I'm so angry
I'll jump up and down • I'll roll on the ground
Make a din • Make you spin
Pull out my hair • Throw you in the air
Pull down posts • Hunt down ghosts
Scare spiders • Scare tigers
Pull up trees • Bully bees
Rattle the radiators • Frighten alligators
Cut down flowers • Bring down towers
Bang all the bones • Wake up stones
Shake the tiles • Stop all smiles
Silence birds • Boil words
Mash up names • Grind up games
Crush tunes • Squash moons
Make giants run • Terrify the sun
Turn the sky red • And then go to bed.

INSIDE OUT

Inside out
Outside in
You can't lose
I can't win.

I've got a sausage
You've got a pie
I can't whistle
And I don't know why.

I've got a letter
You've got a phone
You like sandwiches
I like to moan.

Moan,

moan

Moan,

moan

Moan,

moan

Moan,

moan.

NAUGHTY CAR

I'm very cross with you.

You've gone too far.

You can do better.

You're a very naughty car.

You know what I mean.

Are you ashamed of yourself?

If this happens again,

You're going back on the shelf.

ARE YOU LISTENING?

Are you listening?

Don't play with your food.

Don't answer back

And don't be rude.

If you burp

You know you say "pardon."

If you don't

I'll put you in the garden.

You're asking for trouble

I don't believe it.

The food's on the table

Eat it or leave it.

Don't start laughing

Did you hear what I said?

Do what I say

Or you're going to bed.

45

I don't want the jelly

'cause the jelly's too smelly

I don't want the ducky

'cause the ducky's too yucky

I don't want the drink

'cause the drink is too stinky

And I don't want the sick

'cause the sick is too sicky

47

OH DEAR

I went to the shop
To get me a carrot
Oh dear!
They gave me a parrot.

Oh dear!
Look what I got
Do I want that?
No I do NOT!

I went to the shop
To get me a hat
Oh dear!
They gave me a cat.

Oh dear!
Look what I got
Do I want that?
No I do NOT!

I went to the shop
To get me a cake
Oh dear!
They gave me a snake.

Oh dear!
Look what I got
Do I want that?
No I do NOT!

I went to the shop
To get me some juice
Oh dear!
They gave me a goose.

Oh dear!
Look what I got
Do I want that?
No I do NOT!

I went to the shop

To get me a chair

Oh dear!

They gave me a bear.

Oh dear!

Look what I got

Do I want that?

No I do NOT!

I went to the shop

To get me some peas

Oh dear!

They gave me some bees.

Oh dear!

Look what I got

Do I want that?

No I do NOT!

I went to the shop

To get me a truck

Oh dear!

They gave me a duck.

I went to the shop

To get me some pants

Oh dear!

They gave me some ants.

Oh dear!

Look what I got

Do I want that?

No I do NOT!

Oh dear!

Look what I got

DO I WANT THAT? NO I DO I DO NOT!

GRUFF AND DAVE

GRUFF

Gruff was a **grumpy** dog.
Gruff was very **grumpy**.
Other dogs made him jump,
So Gruff was very jumpy.

Dave was a jumpy frog.
Dave was very jumpy.
Other frogs made him cross,
So Dave was very **grumpy**.

So Gruff was **grumpy** and jumpy.
A **grumpy**, jumpy dog.
Dave was jumpy and **grumpy**.
A jumpy, **grumpy** frog.

One day in a garden in Kew
Gruff met Dave the frog.
They met on a cold winter's day
Dave and Gruff the dog.

DAVE

They walked around in the mud.
The mud was **bumpy** and **lumpy**.
They rolled around in the mud,
And they got to be **lumpy** and **bumpy**.

So now they meet every day,
And Dave isn't so **grumpy**.
They meet in the mud at Kew,
And Gruff isn't so jumpy.

Now Dave is **bumpy** and **lumpy**,
Not **grumpy** but still very jumpy.
And Gruff is **bumpy** and **lumpy**,
And he's not jumpy or **grumpy**.

M O

Mo's in a muddle

She slipped in a puddle

Mommy gives Mo

A great big cuddle.

AN ACCIDENT

You fell off the table

And landed on your head.

I picked you up

And put you to bed.

You had a little sleep

Your head was very sore

You've got a big head

Is it hurting anymore?

WINTER

When it was winter

I got a splinter

Then my sister

Got a blister

Then my brother

Got another

You got a splinter

Your sister got a blister

Your brother got another

Said my mother.

59

WE CAN

We can do what a bumblebee does
Buzz buzz buzz, *buzz buzz buzz*

We can do what brown cows do
Moo moo moo, *moo moo moo*

We can talk like parrots talk
Squawk squawk squawk, *squawk squawk squawk*

We can sing like doorbells sing
Ring ring ring, *ring ring ring*

We can hoot like cars hoot
Toot toot toot, *toot toot toot*

We can wash like you wash
Splosh splosh splosh, *splosh splosh splosh*

We can grumble like teddies grumble
Mumble mumble mumble, *mumble mumble mumble*

LET ME DO IT

Let me do it, let me do it

Let me blow up the balloon

Let me do it, let me do it

Let me go to the moon

Let me cook the beans

Let me lick the jar

Let me kick the ball

Let me drive the car

Let me do it, let me do it

Let me blow up the balloon

Let me do it, let me do it

Let me go to the moon

Let me drive the beans

Let me kick the jar

Let me lick the ball

Let me cook the car

Let me do it, let me do it

Let me blow up the balloon

Let me do it, let me do it

Let me go to the moon

Let me kick the beans

Let me drive the jar

Let me cook the ball

Let me lick the car

Let me do it, let me do it

Let me blow up the balloon

Let me do it, let me do it

Let me go to the moon

A SLOW TRAIN, GETTING

I'm a very, very, very slow train,

And I'm very, very late again.

I should be there at half past seven.

I won't be there till half past eleven.

You've never, ever seen

A train this slow.

Never, never, never, never

Never, never, no.

SLOWER AND SLOWER

COMING HOME

Here's a house

Here's a door

Here's a ceiling

Here's a floor

Here's a wall

Here's the stairs

Here's a table

Here's the chairs

Here's a bowl

Here's a cup

Open your mouth

And drink it up.

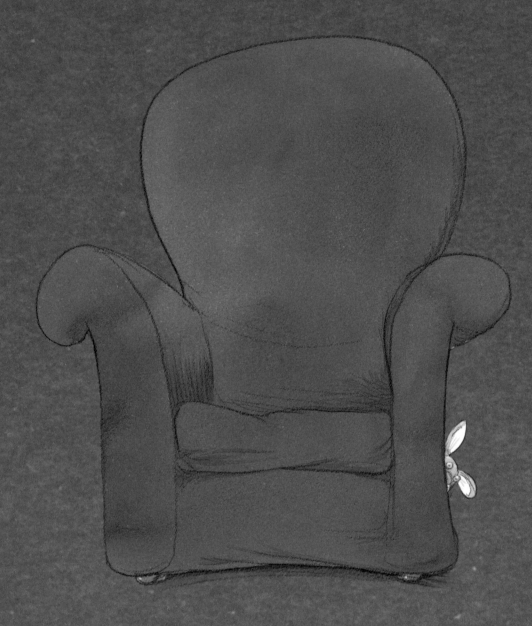

You can't see me

You don't know where I am

Am I in the paint pot?

Am I in the jam?

Am I in the sink?

Am I in the train?

Am I in the drawer?

Am I in the plane?

Am I on the shelf?

Am I in a book?

Am I in the bed?

Go and have a look.

Am I under the table?

You're getting very near.

I can see you.

I'm sitting over here.

YOU FOUND ME!

HELLO GOOD-BYE

Hello, Dolly

Hello, Solly

Hello, Molly

Hello, Holly

Hello, Wally

Hello, Ollie

How do you do?

We're OK

How are you?

Do you know what?

I'm OK too.

Dolly

Solly

Holly

Wally

Good-bye, Dolly

Good-bye, Solly

Good-bye, Molly

Good-bye, Holly

Good-bye, Wally

Good-bye, Ollie.

Good-bye, you!

Molly

Ollie

First U.S. edition 2015

Library of Congress Catalog Card Number 2014954537
ISBN 978-0-7636-8116-6

15 16 17 18 19 20 APS 10 9 8 7 6 5 4 3 2 1

Printed in Humen, Dongguan, China

This book was typeset in Futura.
The illustrations were done in watercolor and pencil.

Candlewick Press
99 Dover Street
Somerville, Massachusetts 02144

visit us at www.candlewick.com